11/15

Happy Birthday
West!

Love you — Aunt Betsy
and Uncle Matt

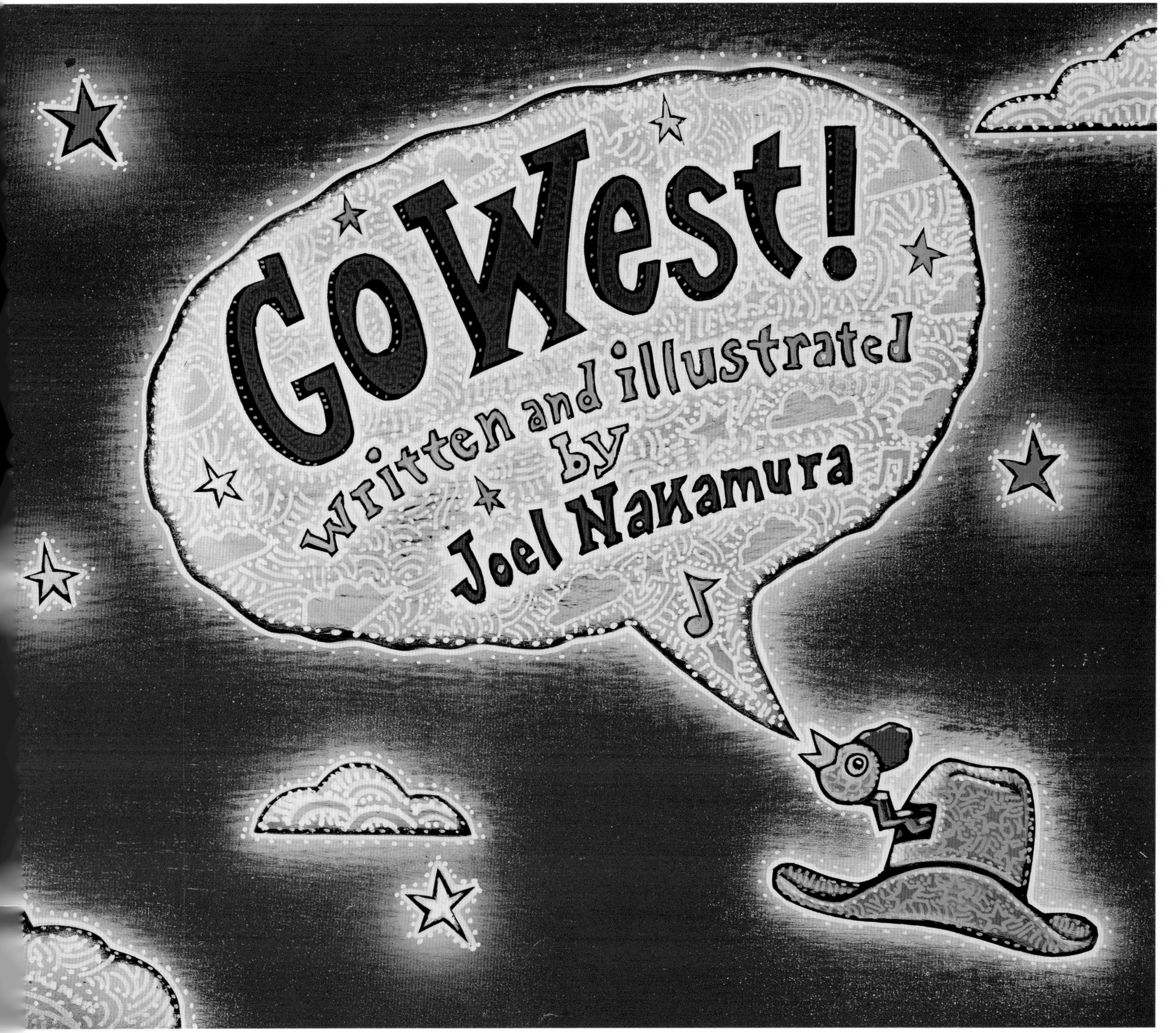
Go West!
written and illustrated by
Joel Nakamura

Where cowgirls have rocket boots
and dancing skirts and cuckoo hats

Where the birds run fast and time runs slow

Go West! Where horses of many colors run

Published by Leaf Storm Press
Post Office Box 4670
Santa Fe, New Mexico 87502
LeafStormPress.com

Leaf Storm Press books are available for special
promotions and premiums. For information, please email publisher@
leafstormpress.com.

ISBN 978-0-9914105-6-9
Library of Congress Control Number: 2015932908

The illustrations in this book were created by hand with brushes and
acrylic paint on metal.

First Edition 2015
Book Design by Maria Levy
Printed in Malaysia

10 9 8 7 6 5 4 3 2

Publisher's Cataloging-in-Publication Data
(Provided by Quality Books, Inc.)

        Nakamura, Joel.
            Go West! / written and illustrated by
        Joel Nakamura.
            pages cm
            SUMMARY: An illustrated tour of the Western
        United States and its unique characteristics.
            Audience: Ages 3-6.
            LCCN 2015932908
            ISBN 978-0-9914105-6-9

            1. West (U.S.)—Description and travel—Juvenile
        literature. 2. West (U.S.)—Social life and customs—
        Juvenile literature. 3. West (U.S.)—Description and
        travel. 4. West (U.S.)—Social life and customs.
        I. Title.

        F595.3.N35 2015   917.804
                                   QBI15-600038